P9-EBY-918

Keeping Your Body Alive and Well

A Children's Book about Physical Needs

by

Joy Wilt

Illustrated by Ernie Hergenroeder

Educational Products Division
Word, Incorporated
Waco, Texas

Author

JOY WILT is creator and director of Children's Ministries, an organization that provides resources "for people who care about children"—speakers, workshops, demonstrations, consulting services, and training institutes. A certified elementary school teacher, administrator, and early childhood specialist, Joy is also consultant to and professor in the master's degree program in children's ministries for Fuller Theological Seminary. Joy is a graduate of LaVerne College, LaVerne, California (B.A. in Biological Science), and Pacific Oaks College, Pasadena, California (M.A. in Human Development). She is author of three books, *Happily Ever After, An Uncomplicated Guide to Becoming a Superparent,* and *Taming the Big Bad Wolves,* as well as the popular *Can-Make-And-Do Books.* Joy's commitment "never to forget what it feels like to be a child" permeates the many innovative programs she has developed and her work as lecturer, consultant, writer, and—not least—mother of two children, Christopher and Lisa.

Artist

ERNIE HERGENROEDER is founder and owner of Hergie & Associates (a visual communications studio and advertising agency). With the establishment of this company in 1975, "Hergie" and his wife, Faith, settled in San Jose with their four children, Lynn, Kathy, Stephen, and Beth. Active in community and church affairs, Hergie is involved in presenting creative workshops for teachers, ministers, and others who wish to understand the techniques of communicating visually. He also lectures in high schools to encourage young artists toward a career in commercial art. Hergie serves as a consultant to organizations such as the Police Athletic League (PAL), Girl Scouts, and religious and secular corporations. His ultimate goal is to touch the hearts of kids (8 to 80) all over the world—visually!

Keeping Your Body Alive and Well

Copyright © 1979 by Joy Wilt. All rights reserved. Printed in the United States of America. No part of this book may be used or reproduced in any manner whatsoever without written permission, except in the case of brief quotations embodied in critical articles and reviews. For information, address Educational Products Division, Word, Incorporated, 4800 W. Waco Drive, Waco, Texas 76710.

ISBN 0-8499-8117-4
Library of Congress Catalog Card Number: 78-66138

Contents

Introduction

Keeping Your Body Alive and Well is one of a series of books. The complete set is called *Ready-Set-Grow!* Keeping Your Body Alive and Well deals with physical needs and can be used by itself or as part of a program that utilizes all of the *Ready-Set-Grow!* books.

Keeping Your Body Alive and Well is specifically for children ages four to eight. Children can either read the book themselves or have it read to them. This can be done at home, church, or school.

Keeping Your Body Alive and Well is designed to involve the child in the concepts being taught. This is done by simply and carefully explaining each concept and then asking questions that invite a response from the child. It is hoped that by answering the questions the child will personalize the concept and, thus, integrate it into his or her thinking.

The body is one of the most marvelous machines known to humankind. It is almost completely self-contained and functions with absolute precision. Indeed, it is one of a person's greatest gifts, and yet often it is mistreated and abused.

Much of the abuse that human bodies receive is a result of ignorance. Many people do not know how to care for their bodies. It is no wonder that so many people (especially Americans) suffer from overweight, heart problems, ulcers, and the like. Humans bring on themselves a great deal of the sickness and disease they experience.

Caring for one's body is a lifetime commitment that should begin during childhood. The educational process that leads to this commitment should begin when a child is very young.

Children should be taught what their bodies need in order to survive and grow and how to go about getting these needs met. This is precisely what Keeping Your Body Alive and Well is all about. It teaches children what their physical needs are and how to get these needs met. It is designed to teach a child that God created him or her a physical being with physical needs. Having physical needs and getting those needs met is part of God's plan for every person. Children who grow up believing and accepting this will be equipped to live healthy, exciting lives.

Keeping Your Body Alive and Well

If you would like to keep your body alive and well. . .

this book is for you.

These are plants.

Plants are living things.

Because plants are living things, they spend their whole lives working to. . .

stay alive and well.

In order to stay alive and well, plants need certain things. Plants need. . .

air and light,

and food and water.

get very sick

and eventually die.

These are animals.
Animals are living things.

Because animals are living things, they spend their whole lives working to. . .

stay alive and well.

In order to stay alive and well, animals need certain things.

Animals that do not receive enough of the things they need. . .

get very sick and may even die.

A person is a special kind of animal. . .

with special needs.

What does a person need in order to stay alive and well ?

Chapter 1

A Person Needs Good Food

Too much of some foods hurts people rather than helps them.

Good food makes it possible for people to stay alive and well.

Every person needs protein. Protein helps the body. . .

grow, become strong
and stay well.

Some foods that give us protein are. . .

milk, cheese, eggs, beef, veal, pork, lamb,
fish, poultry, dried peas, dried beans, lentils,
and nuts.

Every person needs carbohydrates. Carbohydrates
give the body...

energy (the strength or eagerness to work and do things).

Some foods that give us carbohydrates are. . .

fruits, sugar, corn, rice, potatoes, bread, cereal, and noodles.

Every person needs fats.
Fats give the body. . .

energy and certain vitamins.

Fats also keep the skin
smooth and healthy.

Some foods that give us fats are. . .

vegetable oils, cream, butter, margarine,
mayonnaise, and bacon.

Every person needs fiber. Fiber helps the body. . .

digest its food.
It also contributes to
healthy gums and
clean teeth.

Some foods that give us fiber are. . .

raw fruits, vegetables, and whole grain cereals.

Every person needs vitamins. Vitamins help the body. . .

grow. They also regulate the things that the body does, and help prevent certain sickness and diseases.

Some foods that give us vitamins are. . .

milk, eggs, wheat germ, oil, yeast, fruits, vegetables, cereal, meat, fish, liver, and nuts.

Every person needs minerals.   Minerals help the body...

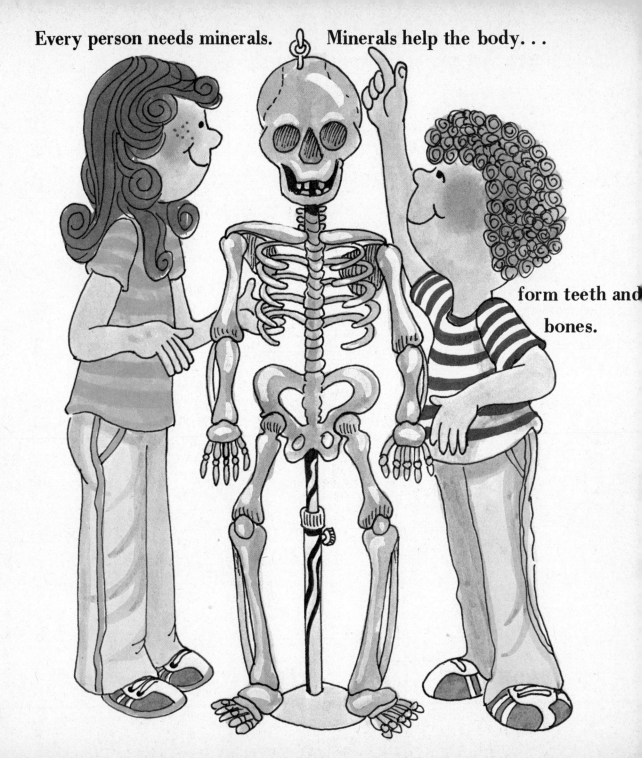

form teeth and

bones.

Some foods that give us minerals are. . .

milk, cheese, eggs, meat, liver, dried fruit, seafood, vegetables (especially the green leafy ones), and salt.

God created your body, and he wants you to keep it alive and well by eating foods that include:

Protein
Carbohydrates
Fats
Fiber
Vitamins
Minerals

To make sure that your body is getting enough of the right foods, you need to eat the following things every day:

2 fruits (one should be a citrus fruit)

2 vegetables (one should be dark green or deep yellow)

3 or more cups of milk

2 or more servings of either cheese, eggs, beef, veal, pork, lamb, fish, poultry, dried beans, dried peas, lentils, or nuts

4 or more servings of whole grain, enriched or restored bread or cereal.

What does a person need in order to stay alive and well ?

Chapter 2

A Person Needs Water, Air, and Sunshine

Every person needs water
because. . .

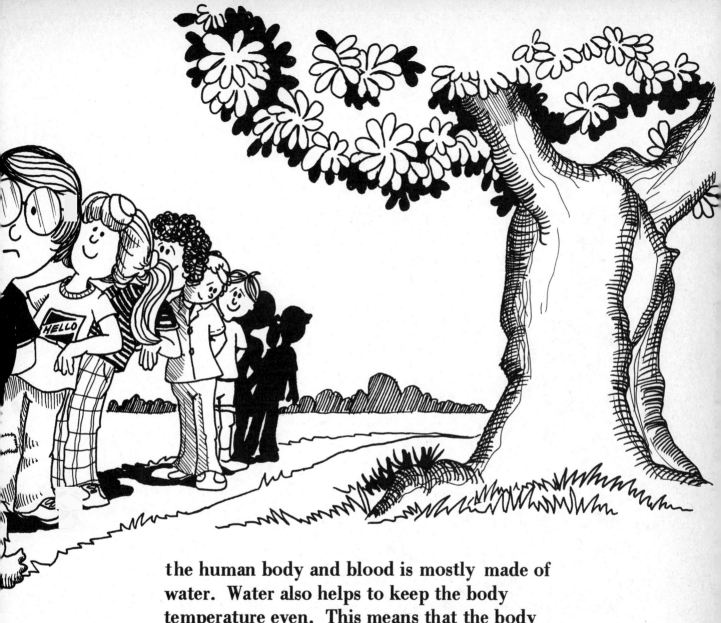

the human body and blood is mostly made of
water. Water also helps to keep the body
temperature even. This means that the body
does not get too hot or too cold.

Every person needs air because. . .

air provides the oxygen that the body needs
in order to change food into energy.

Every person needs sunshine because...

sunshine provides vitamin D which the
body needs in order to make strong teeth
and bones.

God created your body, and he wants you to keep it alive and well by using the:

water

air, and

sunshine

that he has given you.

To make sure that your body is getting enough water, air, and sunshine:

Drink several glasses of water every day.

Work and play outside in the fresh air and sunshine as much as possible.

Do not put anything over your nose or mouth that will not allow you to breathe air (such as plastic bags).

Do not get into anything that will not have enough air for you to breathe (such as refrigerators, freezers, dryers, or closets).

What does a person need in order to stay alive and well?

Chapter 3

A Person Needs Exercise

Exercise keeps the muscles of the body in good shape so that they can move the body. Exercise also helps the blood and other body fluids circulate food, water, and air to every part of the body.

God created your body, and he wants you to keep it alive and well by exercising.

You get some exercise by working and playing, but not enough. When you work and play, you use some of your muscles, but you do not use all of them.

This is why you need to do exercises. If you do the following exercises every day, you can be sure that all your muscles will get the use they need in order to be healthy and strong.

Exercise #1: Toe Touch

1

Stand tall with your feet together or slightly apart and your arms over your head.

2

Keeping your knees as straight as you can, bend forward and touch the floor.

3

Return to your starting position.

Each return to the starting position counts one.

Exercise #2: Knee Raise

1

Stand tall with your feet together and your arms down at your sides.

2

Keeping your back as straight as you can, grab your left knee and shin with your hands.

4

Do the same thing with your right leg.

58

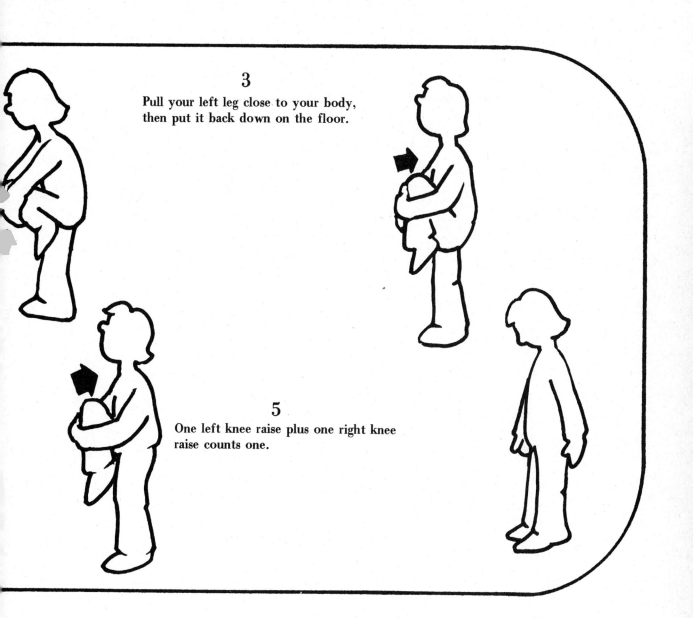

3

Pull your left leg close to your body,
then put it back down on the floor.

5

One left knee raise plus one right knee
raise counts one.

59

Exercise #3: Side Bend

1

Stand tall with your feet about twelve inches apart. Bend your right arm over your head. Put your left hand on the side of your left thigh.

3

Return to your starting position, and change your arms (bend your left arm over your head and put your right hand on your right thigh).

2

Keeping your back and knees as straight as you can, bend sideways.

Move your left hand down your left leg as far as you can. Point left as far as you can with your right hand.

4

One bend to the left plus one bend to the right counts one.

Exercise #4: Arm Circles

1

Stand tall with your feet about twelve inches apart and your arms at your sides.

2

Make backward circles with both arms at the same time, then make forward circles with both arms at the same time.

3

Each full arm circle counts one. Do half of your arm circles backward and half of them forward.

Exercise #5: Rocking Sit-Up

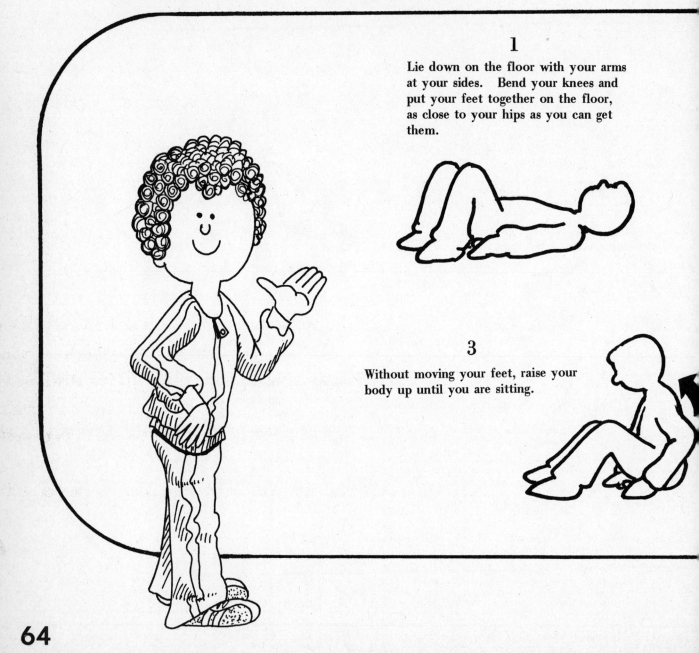

1

Lie down on the floor with your arms at your sides. Bend your knees and put your feet together on the floor, as close to your hips as you can get them.

3

Without moving your feet, raise your body up until you are sitting.

2

Keeping your feet flat on floor, slide them away from your hips as far as you can.

4

Reach down and touch your toes with your fingers.

5

Return to your starting position.

Each return to the starting position counts one.

Exercise[#] 6: Head and Leg Raise

1
Lie face down on the floor with your arms along your sides. Tuck your hands under your legs.

2

Keeping both legs as straight as you can,
lift your head, shoulders, and left leg
as high as you can off the floor.

3

Do the same thing using your right
leg.

Each head-shoulder-leg raise counts one.

Exercise #7: Side Leg Raise

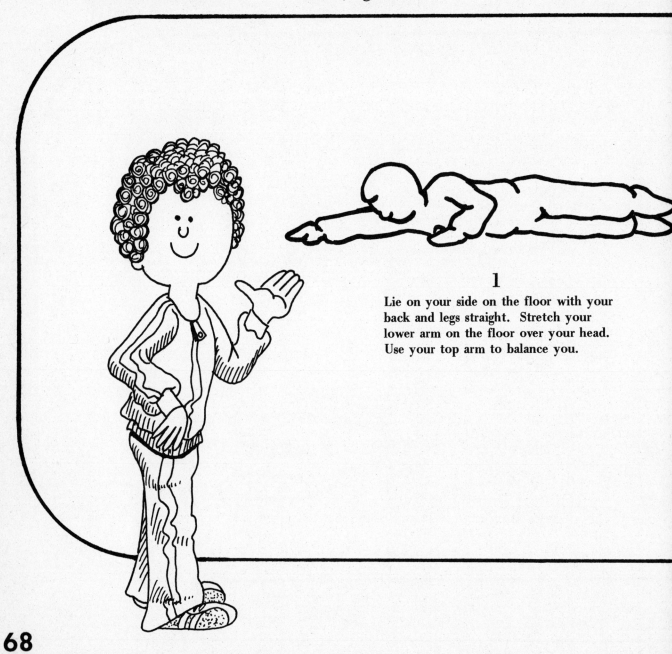

1

Lie on your side on the floor with your
back and legs straight. Stretch your
lower arm on the floor over your head.
Use your top arm to balance you.

2

Raise your upper leg as high as you can,
then put it down again.

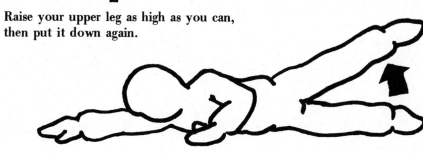

3

Each leg raise counts one. Do half of
your leg raises with your left leg, then
half of them with your right leg.

Exercise[#] 8: Knee Push-Up

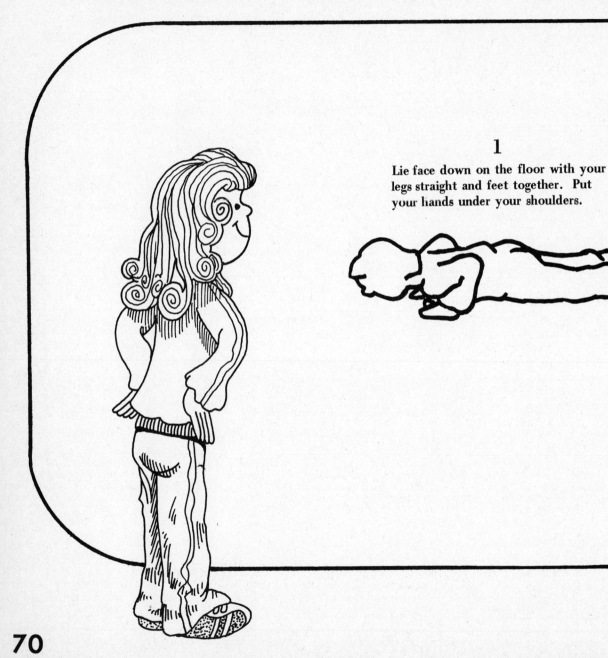

1

Lie face down on the floor with your legs straight and feet together. Put your hands under your shoulders.

2

Keeping your back as straight as you can, and your hands and knees on the floor, push your body off the floor until your arms are straight.

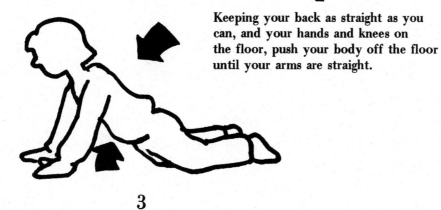

3

Return to your starting position.

Each return to the starting position counts as one.

Exercise[#] 9: Cross Over

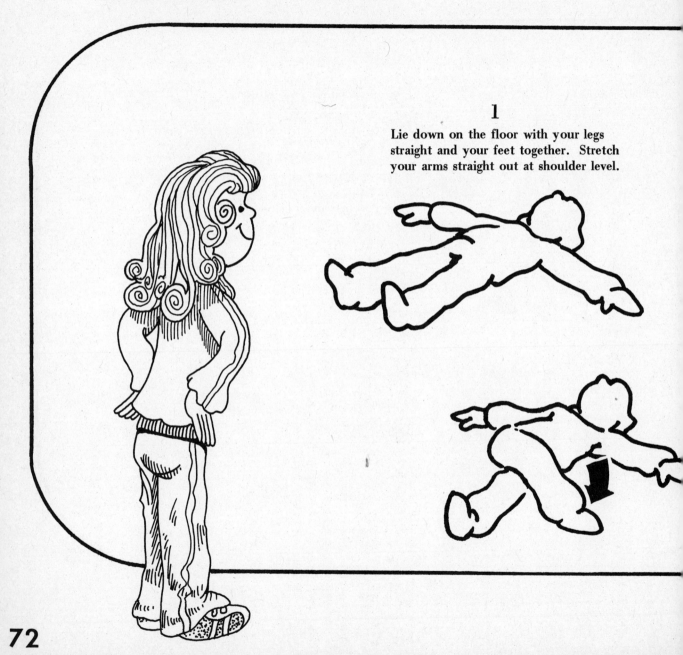

1

Lie down on the floor with your legs straight and your feet together. Stretch your arms straight out at shoulder level.

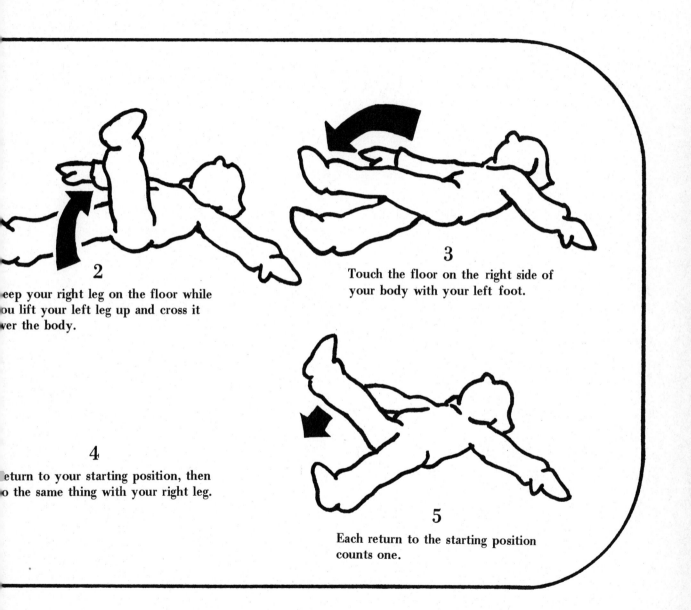

2

eep your right leg on the floor while ou lift your left leg up and cross it ver the body.

3

Touch the floor on the right side of your body with your left foot.

4

eturn to your starting position, then o the same thing with your right leg.

5

Each return to the starting position counts one.

Exercise #10: Posture Exercise

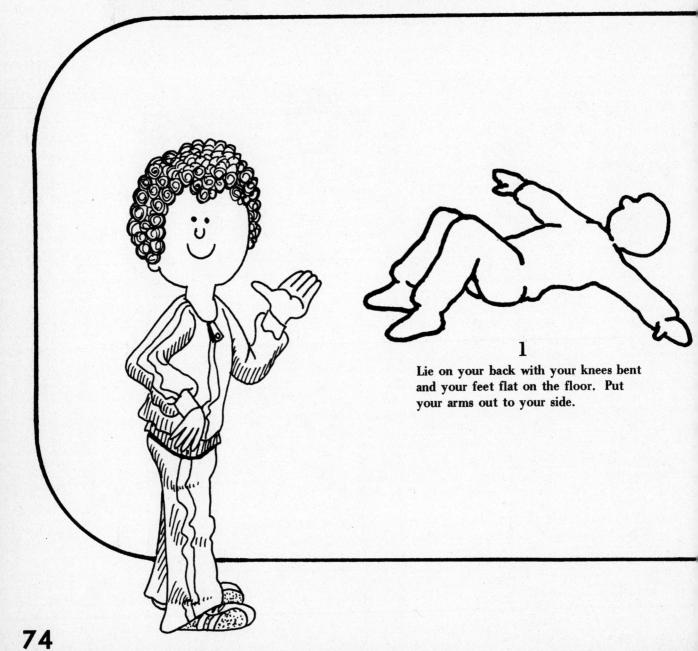

1

Lie on your back with your knees bent and your feet flat on the floor. Put your arms out to your side.

2

Press your back to the floor as hard
as you can and then relax.

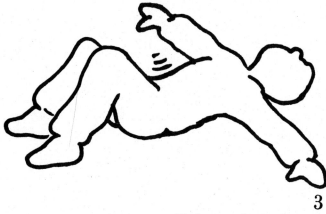

3

Each time the back presses to the floor counts one.

Exercise #11: Foot and Ankle Circles

1

Sit on the floor with your legs straight and your feet about fourteen inches apart. Put your hands on the floor behind you to help you sit up.

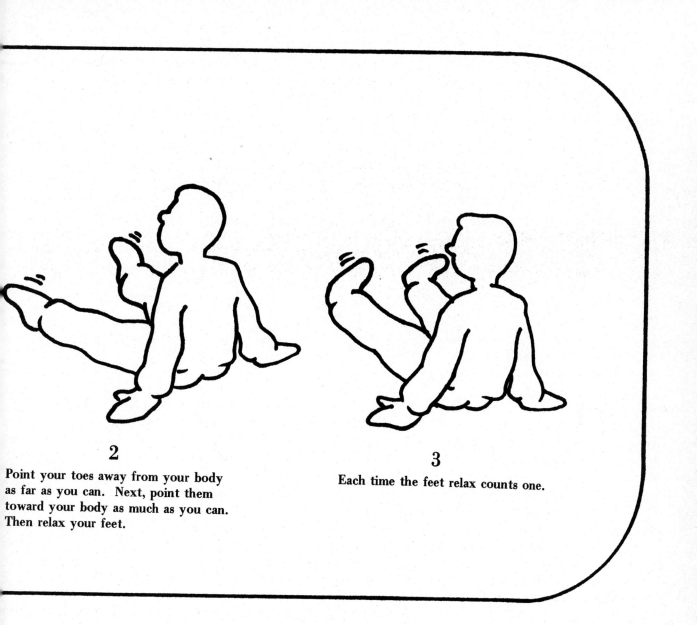

2

Point your toes away from your body
as far as you can. Next, point them
toward your body as much as you can.
Then relax your feet.

3

Each time the feet relax counts one.

Exercise #12: Run and Jump in Place

1

Stand tall with your feet together and your hands at your sides.

2

Run in place.

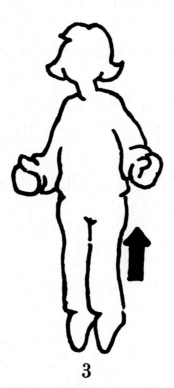

3

Every time your left foot touches the floor counts one. After fifty counts, jump up and down ten times. Keep your legs as straight as you can when you jump.

HERE IS A CHART TO TELL YOU HOW MANY OF EACH EXERCISE YOU SHOULD DO EVERY DAY.

Exercise

DAY	1	2	3	4	5	6
1	3	4	5	18	4	4
2	3	4	5	18	6	4
3	3	4	5	18	8	6
4	5	5	7	18	10	8
5	5	5	7	20	12	8
6	5	5	7	20	14	10
7	7	7	8	20	16	12
8	7	7	8	20	18	12
9	7	7	8	26	20	14
10	9	8	10	26	22	16
11	9	8	10	26	24	18
12	9	8	10	26	26	20
13	10	10	11	28	28	21
14	12	12	12	28	30	22

80

7	8	9	10	11	12
4	3	2	3	4	50
6	3	3	5	5	60
8	4	4	6	6	70
10	5	6	8	7	80
13	6	6	9	8	90
16	7	8	11	10	100
18	8	10	12	11	115
20	9	10	14	13	125
23	10	11	15	14	140
25	12	12	18	16	150
26	13	14	18	17	160
28	14	14	20	18	175
30	14	16	22	19	190
32	16	16	24	22	200

AFTER THE 14th DAY, KEEP DOING THE SAME NUMBER OF EXERCISES THAT YOU DID ON THE 14th DAY. AS YOU GET STRONGER, YOU CAN DO MORE AND MORE OF EACH EXERCISE.

What does a person need in order to stay alive and well ?

Chapter 4

A Person Needs Rest and Sleep

Every person needs rest and sleep because. . .

rest and sleep give the body a chance to get
rid of body waste, repair itself, and grow. They
also allow the body to build up energy.

If the human body does not get enough rest and sleep, a person becomes. . .

cross and cranky.

A tired person often gets sick because. . .

disease germs attack a tired person more
easily than a rested one.

God created your body, and he wants you to keep it alive and well by giving it plenty of rest and sleep.

To make sure that your body is getting enough rest and sleep:

  Take time during the day to sit or lie down and rest your body.
  Sleep at least nine or ten hours every night.

What does a person need in order to stay alive and well?

Chapter 5

A Person Needs to Be Clean

Every person needs to
keep himself or herself
clean because. . .

germs that cause disease and sickness grow in dirt. Dirt also clogs the openings in the skin and hinders it from breathing.

Every person needs to wash his or her entire body
every day because the dirt that contains germs and clogs the openings
in the skin needs to
be washed
away.

Every person needs to wash his or her hair regularly because. . .

dirt from the hair can get in a person's eyes and ears and cause infections.

Every person needs to wash his or her hands before eating food because. . .

dirt containing germs can come off the hands onto the food.

When the food is eaten, the germs get inside the body and can cause disease and sickness.

Every person needs to brush his or her teeth after eating food because. . .

food particles that are left on the teeth can cause the teeth to decay. Decayed teeth cannot cut, tear, and grind food for the body like they are supposed to. Also, germs from decayed teeth may spread disease throughout the body.

God created your body, and he wants you to keep it alive and well by keeping it clean.

To make sure that your body, hair, hands, and teeth are clean:

Take a bath or shower every day.
Wash your hair regularly.
Wash your hands before you eat.
Brush your teeth after you eat.

What does a person need in order to stay alive and well?

Chapter 6

A Person Needs Proper Clothing

Every person needs to wear proper clothing
because. . .

clothing protects a person from the weather.

Every person needs to wear warm clothes when the weather is cold because...

the body must stay warm (approximately 98.6 degrees) so that it will be comfortable and not get sick. If the body gets too cold, it may stop working and die.

Every person needs to wear loose, lightweight clothing when the weather is hot because...

loose, lightweight clothing lets the air get close to the body and cool it.

Every person needs to wear clothing that protects
his or her body from the sun because. . .

the sun can burn the skin and dry up
a lot of the moisture in the body.

Shoes have many purposes. . .

but the main purpose of shoes is to support and
protect the feet. To do this, they should not be
too large or too small. They need to fit just right.

109

God created your body, and he wants you to keep it alive and well by wearing proper clothing.

To make sure that you are wearing the proper clothing:

Wear warm clothes when it is cold.
Wear loose, lightweight clothes when it is hot.
Wear shoes that fit properly.

What does a person need in order to stay alive and well?

Chapter 7

A Person Needs Adequate Shelter

Every person needs to have adequate shelter because. . .

adequate shelter protects a person from rain and lightning.

Every person needs to have adequate shelter
because. . .

adequate shelter protects a person from wind, sleet, hail, and snow.

117

Every person needs to have adequate shelter
because . . .

adequate shelter protects a person from heat and sun.

Every person needs to have adequate shelter because. . .

adequate shelter protects a person from wild
beasts and animals.

121

God created your body, and he wants you to keep it alive and well by taking advantage of the shelter that you have.

To make sure that you are taking advantage of the shelter you have, go inside and stay there if the weather or anything else may harm you in any way or cause your body to get sick.

So how does a person keep his or her body alive and well?

Conclusion

God created you a person, and because he did, your body needs. . .

Good food

Water

Air

Sunshine

Exercise

Rest

Sleep

Cleanliness

Proper clothing

Adequate shelter

so that it can. . .

Stay alive and well.